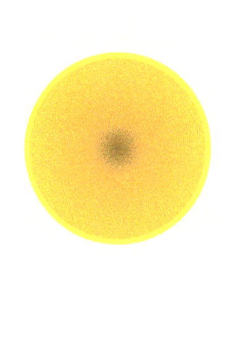

Hugz and His Friend Bugz

Numbers
and
Counting

Copyright © 2015 by Angelina Dunbar

All rights reserved.
No part of this book may be reproduced or used without prior written authorization and the signed consent of the author.

[Hardcover]
ISBN: 978-0-692-55782-2

10 9 8 7 6 5 4 3

Printed in the U.S.A.

www.tales4kids.com

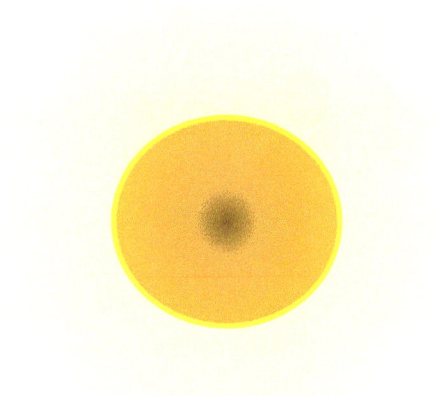
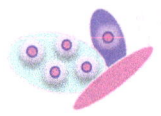

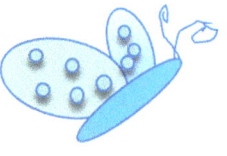

Dear Reader,
This book is dedicated to you.
I hope you like learning numbers and counting and will read more books.

I'm Hugz.

I'm a blue caterpillar.

I'm Bugz.

I'm a ladybug.

Hugz counts...

1

2

3

One Tree   1

Two Bees    2

Three Fleas   3

His friend Bugz counts...

One 1

Two 2

Three 3

Oh no, I don't like fleas!

Hugz counts…

4

5

6

Four Sticks  4

Five Chicks  5

Six Bricks  6

His friend Bugz counts…

Four 4

Five 5

Six 6

Is your house made of bricks?

Hugz counts...

7

8

9

Seven Trains  7

Eight Cakes  8

Nine Swine  9

# His friend Bugz counts...

Seven 7

Eight 8

Nine 9

I wish I could have cake all the time.

Hugz counts...

10

Ten Pens 10

His friend Bugz counts…

Ten 10

Let's count again.

Hugz counts...

1 2 3

4 5 6

7 8 9

10

Numbers and counting are fun!
Too bad we're all done.

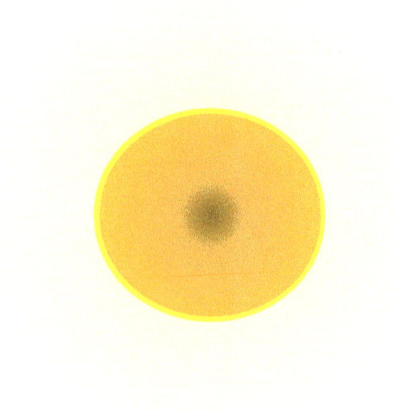
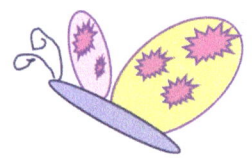

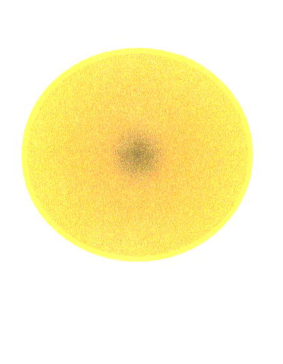

www.ingramcontent.com/pod-product-compliance
Lightning Source LLC
Chambersburg PA
CBHW061403160426
42811CB00100B/1439